CLIFFORD GOLDSTEIN

SHADOW MEN

— A PLAY —

Printed and published by
Signs Publishing Company
Warburton, Victoria

Inquiries concerning performance rights in *Shadow Men*
should be addressed to Signs Publishing Company,
Warburton, Victoria, Australia, or contact via
<www.signspublishing.com.au>.

This book was
Edited by Nathan Brown
Copyedited by Lindy Schneider
Cover designed by Shane Winfield
Cover illustration by Shane Winfield
Typeset: Universe 10.5/14 pt

ISBN 978 1 921292 68 2

Characters

Jason (45523)

Archie (69691)

Bennifer, Prison Guard

Larry, Jason's Brother

Stokes, Prison Guard

Carlita, Jason's Lawyer

Preacher Mike

Detective Frank Spinolo

Richard Stern, Archie's Lawyer

Warden Ivan

Assorted Prison Guards

Act One

Two sterile prison cells divided by a wall. Prisoners, one in each cell. The cells are somewhat backlit so the prisoners' shadows fall forward into the corridor in front of the cells.

Archie, pacing, glances at the clock in the corridor outside his cell. The clock is counting down, in digital red, and at the beginning of this scene reads "17:00". In the next cell, Jason sits calmly on his bed. Archie walks to the bars, grabs two and, pressing his head between them, calls out.

ARCHIE: What are you doing?

JASON: Nothing.

ARCHIE: Nothing? With only 17 hours left?

JASON: What should someone with only 17 hours left be doing?

ARCHIE: Anything but nothing!

JASON: Nothing is something.

ARCHIE: No, nothing is nothing!

JASON: Whatever you say, Archie.

ARCHIE: How can you be so peaceful?

JASON: My conscience is clear.

ARCHIE: You shot a 19 year old in the back of the neck while sipping a chocolate milkshake — and your conscience is clear?

JASON: He was sipping the milkshake, not me. And it wasn't chocolate. It wasn't even a milkshake.

ARCHIE: Stop playing games.

JASON: You have three months, I have 17 hours. Who should be telling whom what to do?

ARCHIE: OK, OK . . . Look, maybe this is selfish, but if you could spare five minutes of your remaining 17 hours to explain the secret of your serenity, I would appreciate it. Even though I used to be a philosophy professor and all that, in the five years we have been next to each other I have never understood it and . . .

The lights flicker. Jason gets up and walks to the bars. Both men look upward.

ARCHIE: 22667?

JASON: No, 44568. 22667 was yesterday.

ARCHIE: Oh, yeah, that's right.

JASON: Was like this the last election year, remember?

ARCHIE: Of course. That's why I don't think they'll do those DNA tests my lawyer has been pushing for. The masses want blood. *(He eases his face from the bars but still*

clutches them in his hands.) Can I ask you
a question?

JASON: You're more capable of answering that than
I am.

ARCHIE: Aren't you scared?

JASON: Scared?

ARCHIE: Yeah, scared? I mean you're about to be
strapped into an electric chair and fried
with 2000 volts. Isn't that frightening?

JASON: I wouldn't know.

ARCHIE: The thought, isn't the thought scary?

JASON: I suppose.

ARCHIE: You suppose?

JASON: Yeah.

ARCHIE: How can you be so calm?

Jason, assuming a smug silence, seems to float onto his bed.

JASON: I can't explain any more, except what I've
always said.

ARCHIE: I know, I know. *(Archie imitates him.)* The
purpose of life is to love and to give some
of yourself for others. Once you do that,
you'll have peace and blah, blah, blah.

JASON: You have the words down, anyway.

3

ARCHIE: OK, so you live for others, right?

JASON: Right.

ARCHIE: And?

JASON: And what, Archie?

ARCHIE: *(Emphatically.)* You love and give of yourself for others—and then what?

JASON: *(A big smile splits his chin from the rest of his face.)* Nothing.

ARCHIE: Nothing?

JASON: Nothing.

ARCHIE: *(He hisses in disgust.)* Ridiculous.

JASON: I said you wouldn't understand.

ARCHIE: Fine, just fine, so I don't understand . . . And maybe you're not scared, but I am.

JASON: Try not to think about it.

ARCHIE: Try not to think about it? That's rich, man, that's rich. Three months away from the chair—and I'm not supposed to think about it? I'm going to remember that one for a long time. *(He lets out a bitter laugh.)* Or at least for three months.

JASON: Relax.

ARCHIE: Yeah, sure. Let's just chill out. Maybe we can ask Warden Ivan to get us a Swedish masseuse, someone to work out that crick in my neck. And maybe I can get liposuction. Don't want my belly ruining the aesthetics of the chair, eh? And a hair implant, too. Who wants a bald, fat electrocuted corpse with a crick in its neck?

JASON: You don't get it.

ARCHIE: No, I don't. *(He almost starts to cry.)* It just doesn't seem right. It just doesn't seem like this is how it should end.

JASON: How should it end, Archie?

ARCHIE: Not like this.

JASON: Not like what? We all wind up dead, so what's the difference?

ARCHIE: I don't understand you.

JASON: I'm going to be dead in less than a day. Why do you need to?

ARCHIE: You can be so frustrating.

JASON: You won't have to put up with it much longer.

ARCHIE: I give up. *(He stretches against the bars, restless, agitated, and waits a few seconds before speaking again.)* Jason?

JASON: Yes.

ARCHIE: Can I ask you a question?

JASON: I believe you are capable.

ARCHIE: It's going to sound a little strange.

JASON: At this point, what does it matter?

ARCHIE: Can I?

JASON: Go ahead.

ARCHIE: May I touch you?

JASON: What?

ARCHIE: I want to touch you.

JASON: What are you . . .

ARCHIE: I mean, all the years in these cells and I've never even shaken your hand. I don't think I've seen your face more than twice and that was so long ago that if I saw you on the street, I'd have to look at your shadow in order to recognise you.

JASON: That's for sure. I don't think I'd know your face if I saw it.

ARCHIE: Maybe we can reach across.

JASON: I don't think it will work.

ARCHIE: Let's try, please.

JASON: OK.

Jason gets up and moves to the front corner of his cell, near the wall next to Archie, who does the same from his side. Both men squeeze their faces into the walls as tightly as possible, reaching their arms through the bars around the wall that separates them. They finally touch and shake hands awkwardly.

ARCHIE: *(Excited.)* We're shaking hands!

JASON: How about that?

ARCHIE: You really are more than a shadow!

JASON: Surprise, surprise!

ARCHIE: Don't let go yet!

JASON: You're about to break my fingers.

ARCHIE: I don't want them to take you, Jason. It isn't right.

JASON: You're crushing me.

ARCHIE: I won't let them!

A prison guard enters. The men pull their hands back into their cells and both men stand tall. The guard walks over and stands before Jason's cell.

PRISON GUARD, BENNIFER: 45523?

ARCHIE: No, it's 45522. Can't you tell 45522 from 45523?

BENNIFER: Shut up—

JASON: Yes, sir, 45523 here.

BENNIFER: You have a visitor.

A man comes in, sheepishly, hesitantly. He's in his mid-fifties, balding and rotund. It's Jason's brother, Larry. The prison guard places a chair outside the cell and out of reach of Jason. The man sits once the chair is positioned.

BENNIFER: *(To the visitor.)* You have 10 minutes. Do not move from the seat. Do not approach the prisoner, nor touch him in any manner. The slightest infraction and the visit terminates. Do you understand?

As the man nods, the guard leaves.

JASON: *(Standing by the bars.)* Larry?

LARRY: Yup, Jason, it's me.

JASON: I can't believe it!

LARRY: It's true.

JASON: Wow! This is, well . . . unexpected.

LARRY: I know, but I'm here.

JASON: Yes, yes, you are. Ah . . . how are you?

LARRY: Good, real good.

JASON: Glad to hear that.

LARRY: Yeah, real good.

JASON: Good, good.

LARRY: I know I should have come to visit earlier . . . but my family has been keeping me busy.

JASON: Of course.

LARRY: The twins—what a handful!

JASON: I bet.

LARRY: And my job keeps me on the road a lot, too. I'm all over the place. One day here, tomorrow there, next day somewhere else. Gets a bit wearying after a while, you know what I mean?

JASON: Yeah, sure.

LARRY: Life's so busy nowadays. Just struggling to pay the bills, we barely have time to watch TV any more, you know?

JASON: Sure.

LARRY: We've been following your case, though.

JASON: That's good.

LARRY: Sorry to hear the appeals have run out.

JASON: That's fate, Larry. We have to learn to live with what we can't change.

LARRY: Wow! That's profound. I'll have to remember that. *(He lowers his head, glances around and whispers.)* There's not much time left, is there?

JASON: No.

LARRY: I'm sorry.

JASON: That's the way things go sometimes.

LARRY: Been hard on the family, as you can imagine.

JASON: I can.

LARRY: The twins—they don't know nothing. Marge and I have worked real hard to keep it from them. They don't ask about their Uncle Jason any more. I don't think they even remember you.

JASON: That's good.

LARRY: I'm glad you understand. I told Marge you would.

JASON: Marge, she's OK?

LARRY: Good, real good.

JASON: Good.

LARRY: Yeah.

JASON: You're looking fine, Larry.

LARRY: Thanks. Been getting a little thick in the middle, you know?

JASON: It happens.

LARRY: Not enough exercise. Life keeps folks too busy. You don't even have enough time to exercise any more. It's crazy.

JASON: Yeah, sure.

LARRY: Of course, I do eat a lot of those fried cinnamon sticks at the mall. You remember how much we used to love them?

JASON: Yes, Larry.

LARRY: Deep fried, coated in sugar and cinnamon. Ummm! I must eat 10 a week. They are so crunchy, so sweet, so rich. I know they aren't good for me—the fat and all—and Marge complains a lot, but we all gotta go somehow, right?

JASON: Right.

LARRY: Yeah, we all do.

JASON: Look, Larry, however short my time is, yours with me is even shorter. Was there anything you wanted to say, or is this simply an older brother coming to pay his last respects to his little brother?

LARRY: Yeah, that's what it is—an older brother coming to pay his last respects to his younger brother. *(He glances around.)* You've been in here a long time.

JASON: More than five years.

LARRY: Has it been that long?

JASON: Afraid so.

LARRY: It seems like just yesterday. Time has a way of going by so fast, doesn't it?

JASON: It can.

LARRY: I mean, it just seems like yesterday we were hunting with Jeff and his crazy dog. Remember how he bragged and bragged about that dog. And then, that first time out, he shot a duck, and sent the dog after it and . . . it ate the duck! *(Laughing hysterically.)*

JASON: *(Smiling, but not sincerely.)* Yes, dogs do that.

LARRY: I'll never forget it. *(He looks at his watch.)* Wow, time goes by so fast.

JASON: We've already established that.

LARRY: Yeah, well, there is one thing I did want to tell you.

JASON: OK.

LARRY: It's not easy and part of me thought about not bothering you, but something inside made me feel I ought to. Plus, Marge insisted, so here I am.

JASON: Thank Marge for me.

LARRY: But I'm real glad I came because it's good to see you again.

JASON: I am glad you came, too.

LARRY: You look great, Jason. Prison seems to have agreed with you.

JASON: Thanks.

LARRY: You're welcome.

JASON: What did you come to tell me?

LARRY: It's about Sally, your wife—your ex-wife.

JASON: I know who she is.

LARRY: I don't know how much you kept in contact with her.

JASON: We've had no contact, at my insistence.

LARRY: That's right, I forget. That was mighty noble of you—giving her the divorce, giving up your rights as a father to the kid. I mean, to try and give them a whole new start and all, with nothing like your murder conviction holding them back. You were real generous in all that.

JASON: You have only another few minutes, Larry.

LARRY: Yeah, well, I don't know all the details. The paper didn't really say much about it.

JASON: As in the newspaper?

LARRY: As in the newspaper.

JASON: What happened?

LARRY: Like I said I don't know the details, but things—things weren't going so good for her. I mean, it started out real good. She had all that money you gave her. And that little house you got her. You remember that?

JASON: Of course.

LARRY: And she was working, only part-time, so she could spend more time with the baby. Just as you had arranged for her.

JASON: Go on.

LARRY: But she started going crazy, again, Jason. Like she always was. Drinking, spending money like mad, you know. Marge and I, we would talk to her and try to put some sense into that pretty head, but once these women get notions to do something, there's just no reasoning with them. I thought Marge was stubborn. She was daisies compared to Sally—

JASON: What happened?

LARRY: Finally she just cut us off. Even sold the house and we couldn't find her or the kid. Then we heard that she was back into drugs and had moved to the city. I tried, Jason, I really tried to track her down. Things must have gotten bad, really bad. I still think it was an accident, you know.

JASON: Accident?

LARRY: I mean . . . I mean I don't think she meant to do it, though it was ruled a suicide.

JASON: Sally committed suicide?

LARRY: That's what the police said, but I don't think so. I really, really don't think so—

JASON: Suicide?

LARRY: I think it was an accident. Drug overdose—
I don't think she would've committed
suicide, Jason . . . do you?

Jason drops to his knees, his face falling against the bars.

LARRY: But the little girl, she's OK. She's so cute.
Jason, you'd be so proud. Don't look like
you much, kind of has this Chinese look to
her and all, but she's like a little doll. And
smart as the day is long. And that's why
we'd like to take her in ourselves, but—

The guard steps over and signals to Larry that time is up. Larry moves toward his brother but the guard stops him and leads him offstage as he stares at Jason, who's on his knees, his face pressed into the bars. Sounds like a small animal being tortured squeeze out of Jason's throat. Archie pushes his face against the bars, trying to see Jason but can't. He looks at the floor, where he sees Jason's shadow instead.

ARCHIE: Jason?

Jason moans, then slams his head against the bars.

ARCHIE: (Seeing Jason's shadow, he speaks gently.)
Take it easy, man.

Jason starts to cry.

ARCHIE: It's going to be OK.

Jason's face is still pressed against the bars. The words "No! No! No!" come out smothered amid sobs. He seems oblivious to Archie. After a minute of these sounds, Jason begins to calm down, though his face remains pressed into the bars.

ARCHIE: Take it easy!

The sobbing stops. Jason sits on the floor of his cell, motionless, as if in a trance. He then jumps up, grabs both bars and squeezes them, his face and body contorting. Archie watches the shadow on the floor.

ARCHIE: What are you doing?

Jason squeezes the bars, grunting, his face turning red.

ARCHIE: Jason, what are you doing?

Still gripping the bar, Jason starts breathing loudly and deeply. It comes out as a hissing between his teeth.

JASON: Suicide? Sally committed suicide?

ARCHIE: Calm down. OK, so she committed suicide. Get a grip.

JASON: I'm dying for a suicide?

ARCHIE: What are you talking about?

JASON: She's killed herself . . . and—and I'm heading to the chair!

ARCHIE: Calm down.

JASON: This is too much—too, too much!

ARCHIE: I'm missing something here.

JASON: Oh, you're missing a lot—a whole lot . . .

He falls face first into the bars, hard enough for Archie to hear.

ARCHIE: What's going on?

JASON: *(Muttering.)* Suicide? Sally committed suicide? This is one nasty joke. Even I couldn't have thought of something this mean. . . . The Big Guy upstairs must be hooting over this one.

ARCHIE: Jason?

JASON: *(Starting a dialogue with himself.)* I'm dying for her in less than 17 hours—and now she's dead? Is that what I'm now facing? *(He laughs.)* Yes, Jason, that's what you are facing. Oh boy, isn't that an unfortunate turn of events? My, yes, it really is, Jason. The innocent dying for the dead, how nice! Oh, but don't worry, everything will work out—

ARCHIE: What are you talking about?

JASON: Just what I said. The innocent dying for the dead!

ARCHIE: Innocent? Who's innocent?

JASON: Me, Jason Bartello, 45523 death row, your fellow, about-to-be-fried shadow!

ARCHIE: Innocent?

JASON: As a newborn baby!

ARCHIE: Innocent? How can you be innocent?

JASON: That's easy—by not doing it.

ARCHIE: By not doing it? What do you mean "by not doing it"?

JASON: I mean not doing it by "not doing it." Is that simple or what?

ARCHIE: But you confessed years ago!

JASON: People do lie, don't they? Oh, yes, they do!

ARCHIE: Innocent? You're saying that you are . . . innocent?

JASON: As a newborn baby!

ARCHIE: Wait a minute, wait a minute . . . The innocent dying for . . . the dead? Sally, she, she . . . ?

JASON: My, my, you are the philosopher extraordinaire, aren't you?

ARCHIE: She did it?

JASON: Two shots, point-blank, in the back of the neck. I knew she had a mean streak but—

ARCHIE: You're kidding me? *(He tries to feign a laugh but it doesn't work.)*

JASON: Do I seem in the joking mood? *(He bursts out in laughter.)* Do I? Do I?

ARCHIE: Wait a minute, wait a minute!

JASON: Yes, Archie, I'm waiting, though every minute's precious, you know, when you don't have many left.

ARCHIE: If this is some last-minute gambit on your part to spare yourself from the chair, then you should have tried it a year before you're going to die, not less than a day.

JASON: Oh yeah, of course, that's exactly what this is. My brother and I had it all planned. Larry's a lot smarter than he looks. But how stupid of me to think I could have fooled you, especially since you have all the power to free me.

Jason falls into the bars again. Light sobs start coughing out of him.

ARCHIE: I can't believe this. You're innocent? You weren't involved?

JASON: I didn't even know about the murder until I read it in the paper.

ARCHIE: But—the confession? Why? I mean, why did you confess?

JASON: I don't know.

ARCHIE: You don't know? *(Archie walks along the bars of his cell.)*

JASON: No.

ARCHIE: This is crazy. It's like I'm looking at your shadow—only it's someone else's. You're saying that you confessed to a murder you didn't commit?

Jason nods his head and Archie sees the shadow nodding.

ARCHIE: Why?

JASON: I said, "I don't know."

ARCHIE: You don't know?

JASON: No. I mean, all I know is that the moment I did, the moment I confessed, I felt this sense of, well . . . goodness.

ARCHIE: Goodness?

JASON: Yeah, goodness. It was like—like for the first time in my life I did something for someone else, with nothing to gain for myself. And it was the most beautiful feeling I ever had.

ARCHIE: What?

JASON: It's hard to explain, but it was like—like every day of my pathetic existence I felt like I was living for nothing—and I mean, nothing. Everything seemed empty, purposeless. No matter how great a businessman I was, no matter how much education I got, no matter the money I made, it all just seemed so pointless until . . .

ARCHIE: Until?

JASON: Until that moment I took the rap for Sally.

ARCHIE: And then?

JASON: And then—for the first time in my life, I felt I meant something. I felt a purpose to my life. I felt a—

ARCHIE: Oh, come off this Mother Teresa stuff. You did it for your kid, so she'd have a mum.

JASON: My kid? You heard my brother. She looks Chinese or something.

ARCHIE: She isn't yours?

JASON: Are you kidding me? I didn't even know Sally was pregnant when I confessed.

ARCHIE: This is crazy.

JASON: Yeah—but that made it even better, Archie. Anyone will do just about anything for their own, but to give of yourself so completely for someone you don't even know? Suddenly there was something inside me, places filled like they never had been before. It was like I discovered the meaning of life—or something. Only, only now . . .

He drops to his knees and starts sobbing again. Bennifer enters and stares at Jason. After a few seconds, he looks at Archie.

BENNIFER: *(Above the sniffles and cries.)* What's happening? What's happening to 45523?

ARCHIE: He's going to die for a crime he didn't commit.

BENNIFER: So who isn't? . . . Hold on there! 45523 confessed. I thought that's why he was always so calm, so happy, like he had made peace with himself.

ARCHIE: Didn't we all?

BENNIFER: I'd sometimes find it more peaceful talking to 45523 than being at home. I learned stuff from him, I really did.

ARCHIE: Didn't we all?

Bennifer walks over and places a hand through the bars, gently, on Jason's shoulder. Jason, startled, looks up. He stares at the hand. Though sniffling, he stops sobbing.

BENNIFER: What happened to you?

Jason says nothing.

BENNIFER: You've been an inspiration, Jason, like maybe death doesn't have to be all that bad. I worry about dying, because my health ain't so great.

Jason says nothing.

BENNIFER: My heart's like an old, bald tyre. Any

moment, it's gonna go flat, but I learned from you that there can be dignity in facing death.

Jason says nothing. He's still transfixed by Bennifer's hand.

BENNIFER: I always wanted to tell you how much hope you gave me.

Jason gazes up at the guard but still says nothing.

BENNIFER: Some of the other guards, they said it was all fake, that you would come unglued as you neared the end, like all the others. But I said, "No, no, not 45523. Never!"

Jason doesn't move.

BENNIFER: I even bet Hauser 50 bucks that you wasn't going to change because you was for real. Yeah, I said, again and again, "45523, he's for real."

Jason jumps up and Bennifer's hand falls off his shoulder. Jason stares him right in the face.

JASON: You lose.

BENNIFER: *(Steps back, startled.)* Whaaa . . . ?

JASON: You lose.

BENNIFER: No, don't say that!

JASON: You bet on a lie—and you lost. Now, go away and leave me alone.

BENNIFER: Jason, Jason?

JASON: Go away!

Bennifer steps away. His lips start to quiver, as if about to cry. Hunched over, deflated, he turns and leaves. Archie stares at Jason's shadow, which is motionless except for his heavy breathing. Neither prisoner speaks for a few long, tortuous moments. Jason drops his head against the bars.

ARCHIE: That was cruel.

JASON: What?

ARCHIE: That was cruel. You just collapsed that guy's world.

JASON: Like that's my biggest concern in life right now.

Jason starts sobbing gently again.

ARCHIE: Take it easy.

JASON: *(Ignoring Archie's words.)* Look at me. I'm crying.

After wiping his tears with his fingers, he holds his hands through the bars and rubs his fingers, implying their wetness. Archie watches the shadow. Jason steps back and throws himself clumsily on the bed, where he sits, speaking toward the opposite wall. He's calm now.

JASON: Me, crying?

ARCHIE: It happens to the best of us.

JASON: You know the last time I ever cried, Archie?

ARCHIE: No.

JASON: I was 11 years old. I know because it was my 11th birthday. June 16th. I remember it perfectly. It was the last time I ever cried, ever. It was because of my dad. Did I ever tell you about my dad?

ARCHIE: No—well, not much.

JASON: My dad left home when I was about six. Can you believe it? A dad would leave a house with a six-year-old boy?

ARCHIE: It happens.

JASON: I was the youngest and I was always asking when Dad was going to come back. And they always said "Soon"—so I would sit on the front porch of our building and wait for him to come. And when he did, he was going to come take me to the docks and we would go deep-sea fishing. The water was going to be rough, the waves would be splashing over the side, and people would be throwing up. But not my dad and me. We were going to catch—I remember it distinctly—we were going to catch a sailfish.

ARCHIE: A sailfish?

JASON: A big one. Eight feet long! I was going to hook the sailfish, and it was going to be this big shiny fish with a long sleek bill, and it was going to dance on its tail across the waves, and the reel would be humming in my hands. And it would be too much for me, but my dad, with his big tattooed muscles, was going to reel it in.

ARCHIE: You had it all worked out, eh?

JASON: And then it was my birthday, my 11th birthday, and each birthday my expectation grew because he would come back on my birthday, I just knew it.

ARCHIE: Jason—

JASON: We lived not far from the airport and I used to think that when a plane came over, if I saw the shadow that meant my dad was going to be on that jet, and when it landed he was going to come. And, sure enough, that day, on my 11th birthday, a jet flew over and I saw its shadow. I sat there all afternoon, because my dad was coming!

ARCHIE: Jason, don't—

JASON: But soon the sun was setting, and I could hear a police siren and a dog was barking somewhere in the distance and I could smell onions cooking. Then these crows landed on the telephone wire above me.

ARCHIE: Crows?

JASON: Three of them. And it was as if they were mocking me or something, but I tried to ignore them because all the signs were there. Finally, I got up to throw a rock at them, and when I looked up, it hit me.

ARCHIE: What?

JASON: The jet—the jet hadn't landed, Archie, it had taken off. Taken off! It hadn't landed, it flew away . . . I dropped the rock and sat on those steps and cried and cried and cried. I went to bed that night and cried until nothing was left inside—nothing!

ARCHIE: I'm sorry.

JASON: I woke up the next morning to a different world, one where the only person I could trust was myself. And that was the secret of my "success." I asked nothing from anyone. I did it all myself. But after that day, I never cried again for anything or anyone because I kept myself away from everything and everyone.

ARCHIE: That's heavy.

JASON: No, it was light. Living only for yourself is living for the smallest common denominator. It's living for this tiny packet of flesh and bone that was one day going to be gone and so all you were living for meant nothing. It all meant nothing, nothing at all . . . until, until I confessed for Sally. Then, then it all seemed to come together, it all seemed to make sense. *(He shakes his head.)* Only now—only now I know that was all a lie, too.

ARCHIE: It's not the worst thing, living a lie, Jason. Most of the world does.

JASON: Is that supposed to comfort me?

ARCHIE: Why not? Look, I always taught my philosophy students that people can't even agree on what it means to say that something is "true."

JASON: Wonderful.

ARCHIE: And after what's just happened to you, I finally see it!

JASON: See what?

ARCHIE: That we don't have to try and assign meaning to our lives. That's the mistake we make, because we're always building it on speculation, on false hopes. Look at you. You built your hope around some drug-addicted sleaze—and now this happened.

JASON: I built my hope around doing something good, something selfless and sacrificial.

ARCHIE: Please! You built your hope around an emotion, a feeling, that's all. You felt good about what you did, eh? Your little act of selflessness was really no different from someone who gets their drug fix. It made you feel good, that's all.

Jason stirs but says nothing.

ARCHIE: I'm not trying to hurt you, man. Look, your action gave you some comfort, some peace, some good feeling, so what's wrong with that? You have to move on.

JASON: *(Jason snickers.)* Great advice, thanks.

ARCHIE: Find some thought, any thought, any angle that helps you cope—and that's it. There's nothing else. It's all about coping.

JASON: So tell me, how does one cope when two innocent men are about to be executed for crimes they didn't commit? Particularly when you happen to be one of the two?

At Jason's words, Archie's countenance changes. He becomes serious, as if in deep thought. He moves cautiously to the corner of his cell, as close to Jason's cell as possible. Jason, on the bed, watches the shadow curl up in the corner.

ARCHIE: *(Whispering.)* Hey.

JASON: Yeah.

ARCHIE: Come here.

JASON: What?

ARCHIE: Come here.

With a long and impatient breath, Jason gets off the bed and squeezes into the corner of his cell, near Archie.

JASON: What?

ARCHIE: *(Whispering.)* I've been wanting to tell you something for a long time.

JASON: What's that?

ARCHIE: *(Lowering his voice even more.)* I'm guilty. I mean, I really did murder my wife in a carefully planned and premeditated act of sheer jealous rage.

JASON: *(Starting to rise and move away.)* You got me over here to tell me what I've known all along?

ARCHIE: How could you know that? And whisper, will you?

JASON: How could I know that? Please! I didn't believe you any more than did any of the—the . . . what, three juries? Your body language gave it all away.

ARCHIE: *(In an angry whisper.)* You've never seen my body!

JASON: *(Standing in the corner.)* You can read a lot from a man's shadow if you look hard enough.

ARCHIE: *(He starts to unravel out of the tight squeeze in the corner.)* Some friend you are.

JASON: What?

ARCHIE: I said, "Some friend you are."

JASON: You're mad because I didn't believe your lie?

ARCHIE: What are friends for, 45523, if not to believe each other's lies?

JASON: *(Jason drops himself back on the bed.)* So what was I supposed to do, argue with you? Besides, if it made you feel good that I faked it, you should be glad. It helped you cope, so who cares if it was a lie?

ARCHIE: Look, Jason, what are we going to do?

JASON: Do? About what?

ARCHIE: About you—being innocent.

JASON: There's nothing we can do. Besides, I don't want to talk about it. I feel sick, nauseated. I just want to sleep.

ARCHIE: Sleep? How can you sleep with just hours left?

JASON: I'll just close my eyes and fall into the hole within—once you shut up and leave me alone.

Jason lies down and closes his eyes.

(End of Act One)

Act Two

Same scene. Clock reads "7:00" and continues to count down. Jason sits on his bed, staring at the opposite wall. Archie stands at the cell bars, arms hanging through them, as if they're holding him upright.

ARCHIE: What are you doing?

JASON: Nothing.

ARCHIE: Nothing?

JASON: A man with nothing to live for doing nothing. What's the problem?

ARCHIE: But you're innocent!

JASON: Really?

ARCHIE: *(He squeezes himself through the bars as far he can, his face contorted against them.)* What?

JASON: Am I really?

ARCHIE: What do you mean?

JASON: Oh, I didn't kill him—but am I innocent?

ARCHIE: *(Relaxing, he stops squeezing through the bars, though he still hangs in them.)* You had me going there for a minute.

JASON: *(A little excited, he leans forward, inhales and speaks louder.)* Maybe that's why we all die, because none of us are innocent?

ARCHIE: Oh, yeah? Then, then what was my neighbour's daughter guilty of when she died of brain cancer at three? *(At those words, Jason falls against the wall and shakes his head.)* But it's OK to believe that, Jason. It really is.

JASON: Sure.

ARCHIE: It is!

JASON: I know, I know. *(Jason glances at the clock.)* Seven hours. It's a prime number, seven. I like the prime-numbered hours the best.

ARCHIE: Why?

JASON: They seem the longest.

ARCHIE: I'd think you'd like the even hours best.

JASON: Why's that?

ARCHIE: Because they're so easy to divide in half— and if you keep dividing them, half after half after half, it should never reach the zero hour. Just gets closer and closer and closer but should never get there. It's an old paradox.

JASON: But it does anyway.

ARCHIE: Lots of things do things that they shouldn't—
even numbers.

JASON: Even numbers. That's scary.

ARCHIE: Not as scary as you dying for a crime you
didn't commit.

JASON: Drop it, Archie.

ARCHIE: Where is your lawyer?

JASON: My lawyer?

ARCHIE: Who else?

JASON: She's supposed to be coming soon.

ARCHIE: How soon?

JASON: I don't know—soon enough. But don't tell
her anything about what I told you. She's
been devastated enough by my sentence.
Takes it kind of personal, you know.

ARCHIE: You have to tell her!

JASON: Why?

ARCHIE: Why? Are you kidding me? She can help you.

JASON: *(Jason gets up, goes to the bars and grabs
one in each hand.)* Help me?

ARCHIE: Like keep you from dying in the next few
hours.

JASON: The next few hours, the next few years,
what's the difference? Besides, I've been

resigned to my death for so long that life seems almost like an aberration.

ARCHIE: Jason, look at me.

JASON: Huh?

ARCHIE: I said, look at me. Are you looking?

JASON: *(Looking at Archie's shadow.)* Yeah.

ARCHIE: You know who you're looking at?

JASON: What?

ARCHIE: I said, do you know who you're looking at?

JASON: Sure.

ARCHIE: No, you think you do—but you don't.

JASON: OK, so who am I looking at?

ARCHIE: You're looking at an aborted fetus.

JASON: A what?

ARCHIE: That's right. I'm an aborted fetus—who survived the abortion.

JASON: Come on . . .

ARCHIE: No, it's true.

JASON: An aborted fetus? You've never said anything about this before.

ARCHIE: Well, it's not exactly something one gets all nostalgic about, eh? But I'm telling you this for a reason, OK?

JASON: OK?

ARCHIE: You told me about your dad, now let me tell you about mine. How much have I already said about "Daddy Dear"?

JASON: Not much, just that he was rich. Inherited it all or something. Never worked or anything like that.

ARCHIE: What else?

JASON: Lots of wives. Five or six, right? Not all at once, though.

ARCHIE: And?

JASON: Kids, all sorts of kids . . . And that he frittered away the family fortune on heroin and horse racing.

ARCHIE: Cocaine and horse racing.

JASON: Yeah, cocaine.

ARCHIE: OK, now let me tell you something else. When Daddy Dear was in his sixties, he got this woman in her twenties pregnant.

JASON: Your mum?

ARCHIE: He agreed to marry her on one condition— after the marriage, she would abort.

JASON: Abort?

ARCHIE: Imagine that—from the wedding reception to an abortion table. I guess at his age— bless his heart—he didn't want any more kids sucking away his cocaine and trifecta money. Anyway, she agreed.

JASON: Really?

ARCHIE: Sure did, but after the wedding she backed away. Finally, late in the pregnancy, he dragged her to some inner-city quack because no-one in their right mind, especially back then, would perform an abortion so late. I don't know what happened, but much to everyone's surprise, out I came—in one piece! Before someone wrapped me in a plastic bag and put me in a garbage can, my mother grabbed me and held on. *Voila!* Here I am—48 years later! What an entrance, eh?

JASON: How do you know all this?

ARCHIE: Are you kidding me? Whenever angry, Daddy Dear never tired of telling me—"If only that doctor knew what he was doing!" Did wonders for my sense of self-worth, you can be sure. By the time I was 16, I could walk into a room and the light sensor wouldn't go on.

JASON: And your mother?

ARCHIE: The few times I asked her, she just burst out crying. Now, let me ask you a question.

Do you know what the odds are of sur-
viving an abortion?

JASON: I can't imagine.

ARCHIE: It's like all but impossible.

JASON: I would guess.

ARCHIE: You don't need to guess anything. It's almost
all but impossible. So, ideally, I shouldn't
be here.

JASON: OK, so?

ARCHIE: OK, so—so I am really bothered that you're
ready to throw your life away when I find
every moment something to cling on to,
no matter what. *(He grabs the bars and
shakes them firmly.)* Life, Jason, life is
something precious. It's precious, and
we should guard it at all costs.

Jason laughs.

ARCHIE: What are you laughing at?

JASON: Nothing.

ARCHIE: Don't tell me nothing. What are you laughing at?

JASON: It was nothing.

ARCHIE: I heard you. What was it?

JASON: It just struck me as funny, that's all.

ARCHIE: What?

JASON: The phrase, "Life is precious." Kind of funny coming from a man who got himself on death row for murdering his wife.

ARCHIE: Shhhhh!

JASON: Sorry.

ARCHIE: Will you watch it?

JASON: I said I'm sorry.

ARCHIE: I can't believe you. *(Archie looks around, as if to see if anyone is listening.)* Squeeze into the corner. Come on!

Jason, unenthusiastically, goes over. Each man huddles in his corner.

JASON: OK.

ARCHIE: Whisper!

JASON: I am.

ARCHIE: Softer. Now listen to me. I, I loved my wife more than life itself.

JASON: Of course, how obvious.

ARCHIE: But nothing I did pleased her—nothing. I tried to fill her every wish, her every whim, but nothing, nothing satisfied her.

JASON: I once had a dog like that.

ARCHIE: Eventually, she cheated on me. *(He gets louder.)* More than once, too! *(He glances around, then lowers his voice.)* I pled and warned, and pled and warned, but nothing changed. Nothing! I was losing my mind.

JASON: Why didn't you just get a divorce?

ARCHIE: I loved her and no matter how many times I told myself "Enough is enough, get out!" I just couldn't. No matter how much I knew I should, I couldn't.

JASON: So you murdered her instead? That's logical.

ARCHIE: Not so loud! What's wrong with you?

JASON: I wasn't loud.

ARCHIE: Yes, you were. *(Looking around, then lowering his voice.)* One day it finally hit me that nothing was going to change. I just couldn't take it, so . . . *(lowering his voice again)* I figured, if I couldn't have her, no-one would. No-one! *(He's silent, looking around.)* I had it all planned to make it look like her latest squeeze—this Cuban accountant named Juan Vega—had done it. I even got some of his body fluids to be at the scene of the crime. That's why I want those DNA tests so badly.

JASON: You tried to frame an innocent man?

ARCHIE: Innocent? Sleeping with my wife? I had every detail worked out and I would

40

have gotten away with it but for the life insurance policy.

JASON: You took out a life insurance policy on her before killing her?

ARCHIE: We had taken them out for each other years earlier. I just forgot all about it, that's all. When the police discovered I got a cheque for half a million dollars, they got suspicious and things started unravelling. But not fully. My lawyer and one of the cops who investigated her death—a detective named Spinolo—are convinced that Vega did it, and they are still working to nail him and free me. I've told you about all that already, many times. Remember?

Jason pulls himself up by the bars and sits on his bed. Archie watches Jason's shadow disappear from his sight.

ARCHIE: *(Still huddled in the corner.)* Where are you going?

JASON: I don't want to hear any more.

ARCHIE: *(He pulls himself up but stands in the corner, his face pressing against the bars.)* What do you mean, you don't want to hear any more?

JASON: I said that I don't want to.

ARCHIE: Why not?

JASON: You want to know why, Archie? I'll tell you why, but first you have to answer this question.

ARCHIE: What?

JASON: Are you happy?

ARCHIE: What kind of question is that?

JASON: Just answer it. Are you happy?

Pressed into the corner, on his feet, Archie says nothing.

JASON: Just what I figured. Now, let me ask you another question.

ARCHIE: Go ahead.

JASON: What is the purpose of your life?

ARCHIE: The purpose of my life?

JASON: Yeah, the purpose of your life—one of those minor-detail kind of things.

ARCHIE: I don't know.

JASON: You don't know?

ARCHIE: No.

JASON: Just what I figured, too. Now . . . now will you please explain to me why you would let another man die for a crime that you committed—all in order for you to cling to an unhappy life with no purpose?

ARCHIE: *(His arms flailing through the bars.)* Will you be careful!

Jason flinches. He gets up and goes over to the corner near Archie.

JASON: Sorry.

ARCHIE: I'll kill you, I swear!

JASON: I'm sorry, I'm sorry.

ARCHIE: *(Calming down, while looking around.)* Please, be quiet. *(Whispering.)* You're the only one in the world who I trusted with this. Be careful!

JASON: In a few more hours, it will be only you again.

ARCHIE: Maybe you're resigned to dying, but not me.

JASON: OK, OK, I'll be more careful. But you still didn't answer my question.

ARCHIE: Because it's stupid.

JASON: Stupid?

ARCHIE: Stupid, stupid, stupid!

JASON: Oh, really?

ARCHIE: *(Sarcastically.)* Yeah, really. I mean, it's a real mystery why an unhappy man who doesn't have the answers to life still doesn't want to get fried in the electric chair, eh? You don't need to be an Einstein to figure that one out.

Jason lets out a long breath, as if acquiescing to what Archie had just said.

ARCHIE: Come on, man, get real. If every unhappy person who didn't have the meaning of life worked out committed suicide, there would hardly be anyone left to bury them.

JASON: I guess.

ARCHIE: You don't have to guess anything. It's true.

JASON: Fine, fine. Just drop it.

ARCHIE: Look, I want to tell you a story.

JASON: Sure, Archie, tell me a story. I need a story. Make it a lullaby.

ARCHIE: One of my students, an undergrad, wrote a paper. It was during the Nazi terror in Austria, and these brown shirts barge into the home of an old Viennese Jew. Just before they grab him, he reaches in his desk, pulls out something with one hand and dangles it before them. The thugs stop cold. After staring a few seconds, they holster their pistols and walk out.

JASON: What was it?

ARCHIE: Suppose I told you it was nothing but a tiny piece of metal—iron—attached to a strip of fabric that together probably weren't worth three dollars?

JASON: A medal or something?

ARCHIE: The highest-level Iron Cross possible, which he had earned in the previous war. A tiny piece of worthless junk.

JASON: So?

ARCHIE: So nothing has meaning apart from what people give it. In itself that piece of metal had no power to stop those thugs, but because of the meaning that their culture poured into that tiny scrap of metal and fabric, it was as if he had pulled out a gun and blown them away. That is the power of a symbol. If he dangled the same thing before thugs from another culture, they would have laughed in his face before beating it in.

JASON: So?

ARCHIE: So I haven't been able find a meaning to pour into my life that works for me yet. I might never be able to. But I'm now convinced I'm probably better off not even trying. And if that works for me, if that makes me feel better, then that's fine, because the only thing I can know for sure are my feelings.

JASON: Your feelings?

ARCHIE: Yes! *(He places his hands on his head, elbows protruding. Jason can see this motion through his shadow.)* Listen, I know when I have a headache. I might not know what caused it, I might not know what cures it, or how whatever cures it works. Everything beyond me knowing that I feel this pain in my head is pure speculation.

JASON: *(Shaking his head.)* I don't know.

ARCHIE: Don't know what?

JASON: I just need something— *(he bangs the bars with his fists)*—something more solid.

ARCHIE: You want something solid?

JASON: Is that too much to ask for?

ARCHIE: No, but it's a pretty stupid thing for a man so proud of his self-education to ask for. Reality is mostly empty space. The universe is like one atom per cubic centimetre—that's a grain of sand in a football stadium or something.

JASON: But it feels solid.

ARCHIE: You got it! It feels solid, Jason. Beyond that, it's all lies.

JASON: Lies?

ARCHIE: Lies and more lies. So find one that makes you feel good and get on with life . . . well, you know what I mean.

JASON: *(Staring down, deep in thought.)* But—

ARCHIE: But what?

JASON: Lies?

ARCHIE: All the way down.

JASON: But how can something be a lie if there isn't truth to make it a lie?

ARCHIE: What?

JASON: It's like if I say I'm not scheduled to die in less than seven hours, it's a lie, but only because there is the truth that I am scheduled to die in less than seven hours.

ARCHIE: So?

JASON: So if I live my life as a lie, that's only because there's a truth about my life that I'm not living.

ARCHIE: No, well, yes—I mean, now, well . . . Look, we have to do something. Time is running out.

JASON: Just drop it. It's too late.

ARCHIE: No, I can't. We can't just stand here and do nothing.

JASON: Why not?

A prison guard enters.

PRISON GUARD, STOKES: 45523, you have a visitor. *(He pulls out a chair and places it before the cell. He then looks at the visitor.)* You know the rules.

A gangly black woman, carrying a leather briefcase, sits down, but not before pulling the chair a little closer to Jason's cell. She's in her early thirties, attractive and well dressed. She's clutching the briefcase tightly. She looks carefully at Jason before speaking.

CARLITA: Jason?

Staring at the floor, Jason says nothing.

CARLITA: Jason, what's wrong?

He doesn't move.

CARLITA: Are you OK?

ARCHIE: No, he's not!

CARLITA: *(Looking back and forth between Jason and Archie.)* What's going on?

ARCHIE: He's innocent!

CARLITA: Excuse me?

ARCHIE: He's innocent! The confession was a lie! His wife was the murderer!

CARLITA: *(Looking at Archie.)* Why are you saying this?

ARCHIE: Because he is.

CARLITA: What is going on here?

ARCHIE: Jason is innocent. His wife is the murderer!

CARLITA: *(Looking at Jason.)* If you wanted to change

your plea, Jason, you should have done this years ago . . . *(She stares at Jason, then looks to Archie, then stares at Jason again.)* Oh, no!

ARCHIE: Yes! He's innocent! And his wife is dead.

CARLITA: Dead?

ARCHIE: Suicide. His brother just told him.

CARLITA: Wait, wait—

ARCHIE: Jason's dying for the dead—his wife, the murderer!

CARLITA: *(She glances around, then scoots her chair up closer. She speaks softly.)* Why is he saying this, Jason? What is going on here?

Jason doesn't move.

CARLITA: Look at me, please.

He slowly raises his head.

CARLITA: Why is he saying this?

Jason doesn't answer.

CARLITA: I need to know.

ARCHIE: It's true, it's true!

JASON: Yes, Sally is dead.

CARLITA: No, what he said about . . . the confession?

JASON: Does it matter?

CARLITA: Of course it matters.

Jason goes over to his bed and sits. After a few moments, he looks at her.

JASON: Really?

CARLITA: Jason, what is going on here? Why is he saying this?

JASON: How many years have you been married, Carlita?

ARCHIE: *(Pounding the bars.)* Come on, stop the nonsense will you?

CARLITA: What?

JASON: You heard me.

CARLITA: You're asking how long I've been married?

JASON: Yes, how long?

CARLITA: Twelve years. I've been married 12 years.

JASON: Two kids?

CARLITA: Two kids . . . Amy and Peter.

JASON: Yeah, Amy and Peter . . . Now, let me ask you this question. After they electrocute me, how are you going to spend the rest of the day?

ARCHIE: Will you stop!

JASON: *(Yelling through the wall behind him.)* Shut up, Archie! *(He looks back at Carlita.)* Answer me. What will you do for the rest of the day, Carlita?

CARLITA: Jason, please—

JASON: Let me tell you, then.

CARLITA: Jason—

JASON: You'll cry a little—or knowing you, a lot. You'll take the rest of the day off, I'm sure. Go home, cry more. Maybe then spend time with Amy and Peter.

CARLITA: Jason, why—

JASON: Then what? The next day you'll be back at the office. And soon there will be more clients, more briefs, more court appearances. You'll be taking Amy and Peter to soccer games and movies. You and your husband will go out to eat, make love, plan your next holiday—

CARLITA: Please—

JASON: No, I'm happy for you, Carlita, I really am. Taking Amy and Peter to soccer games, making love to your husband . . . that's, that's what life is all about.

ARCHIE: Come on, man!

JASON: And, and once in a while certain things will remind you of me. You know, a smell, a song, whatever, and there'll be some pain, I'm sure.

CARLITA: Jason—

JASON: And then, within a month, two months, you'll be, I don't know, at the hairdresser and some 21-year-old girl with a ring in her nose and a tattoo on her neck will cut your hair too short or maybe dye it a bit off colour, and you'll feel more pain over what she did to your hair than you will feel, at that moment, over me and my death . . .

CARLITA: Stop!

JASON: *(He jumps up and goes to the bars.)* Right, Carlita, right?

She lowers her head and lightly sobs.

JASON: That's how life is. We have to move past what hurts us. So it's OK, Carlita, it really is . . . But just—just don't sit there and tell me it matters.

She continues to weep.

JASON: Hey?

Sniffing, she looks at him.

JASON: Put your hand on my shadow.

CARLITA: Excuse me?

JASON: *(Pointing downward, he steps across the bars so that his shadow rests next to her.)* My shadow, right there. Put your hand on it.

CARLITA: Jason—

JASON: *(Moving his shadow even closer to her.)* The last request of a condemned man, please.

Carlita leans over and places her palm on the shadow's head. She holds it there while looking at him.

JASON: What do you feel?

CARLITA: What do I feel?

JASON: Yeah, what do you feel?

CARLITA: I feel . . . nothing.

JASON: Nothing?

CARLITA: Yes, nothing's there.

JASON: *(He walks away, taking his shadow with him, and drops himself on the bed.)* That's right . . . and in less than seven hours, there'll be even less.

She looks at her palm on the floor, then sits up. Jason stares at the wall on the other side of the cell. There's a long silence before she speaks.

CARLITA: Jason?

JASON: *(Still looking away.)* Yes, Carlita.

CARLITA: Jason, what Archie said, about the confession and all?

Jason still stares at the opposite wall.

CARLITA: Will you look at me, please?

He turns and looks at her.

CARLITA: For seven years, I've worked on the assumption of, of . . . your guilt. And so all this time, I have been trying to save the life of a guilty man, right?

JASON: No. Archie is right. The confession was a lie.

CARLITA: What?

JASON: Sally killed him, not me.

CARLITA: Excuse me?

JASON: My wife killed him, I didn't. The confession was a lie, Carlita—a clear and simple lie.

CARLITA: No, don't say that!

JASON: She killed him.

CARLITA: Stop those words!

JASON: I lied to protect her.

CARLITA: I won't listen!

JASON: But now she's dead, so everything I did was for nothing.

CARLITA: I don't want to hear this!

JASON: And everything you did for me was for nothing as well.

She puts her hands over her ears and shakes her head.

CARLITA: Stop, stop!

JASON: So I'm not a guilty man about to die but an innocent one—

With her hands on her ears, she starts to sing a hymn.

JASON: *(He jumps up and goes to the bars.)* And there's nothing you—

She sings louder.

JASON: —or anyone can do about it. But it doesn't matter, because you and me and Amy and Peter are all going to die anyway, so it doesn't matter!

Still singing and with her hands on her ears, she jumps up, her briefcase tucked under her arm and flees. Jason and Archie both stand there at the bars, neither speaking. After a few moments, Jason speaks.

JASON: What are you staring at?

ARCHIE: *(Still standing at the bars.)* Nothing.

JASON: Nothing? You're staring at my shadow.

ARCHIE: So?

JASON: So why are you staring? I did what you said.

ARCHIE: You sure did.

JASON: So what's with the look?

ARCHIE: Did you do it because you wanted to save yourself, or because you wanted to torment that poor woman?

JASON: Save myself? I'm not trying to save myself . . .

ARCHIE: *(Imitating Carlita, he puts his hands over his ears.)* I don't want to hear this. *(He lowers his hands.)* I'd sell my mother to the devil to get my death sentence commuted to life in prison, and you—you . . .

JASON: And I—what? I just want to get it over with.

ARCHIE: I don't understand you.

JASON: What's to understand?

ARCHIE: This is crazy.

JASON: Let me ask you a question. How many people have already lived and died?

ARCHIE: How am I supposed to know? Billions, I guess.

JASON: Billions?

ARCHIE: Yeah, billions. So what?

JASON: So, don't so many deaths kind of dilute the meaning of each one?

ARCHIE: No!

JASON: I mean, how many have to die until death is finally watered down to mean nothing at all?

ARCHIE: You're crazy.

JASON: No, I'm rational.

Archie steps back to his bed and sits.

ARCHIE: Forget it, man. Just forget it all. I was just trying to help, trying to keep you from dying tomorrow, but it's obviously not doing any good.

JASON: It's too late. I'm as good as dead now. Pulling the switch, that's just a formality.

Jason falls into the bars. He starts sniffling lightly. Archie, hearing him, slowly goes back to the bars and looks at his shadow.

ARCHIE: You OK?

JASON: Wonderful, just wonderful.

ARCHIE: Sorry . . . Words can make us say the stupidest things.

JASON: It's like, like I see no reason to live and yet I'm scared of death. Does that make sense?

ARCHIE: The scared-of-death part does, believe me.

JASON: If only I knew what came after. I think I'm more scared of just not knowing.

ARCHIE: Death is nothing to us.

JASON: What?

ARCHIE: "Death is nothing to us" — it was the saying of an ancient philosopher, who believed there was only atoms and the void.

JASON: Atoms and the void?

ARCHIE: That's it. And once you're dead, there's nothing, no consciousness, no spirit, nothing. Just the void and some dispersed atoms. So death was nothing to him and his followers because nothing came after.

JASON: Is that what you believe?

ARCHIE: I don't believe anything. I only know what makes me feel good — and the hope of some afterlife does. Whether there is one, I haven't the vaguest idea and I don't want to find out anytime soon, either.

JASON: It's crazy. I mean, we can predict every eclipse for the next thousand years, but questions like what happens after death is guesswork.

ARCHIE: Only a God can save us.

JASON: What?

ARCHIE: "Only a God can save us." That was the saying of another philosopher.

JASON: Who?

ARCHIE: Martin Heidegger.

JASON: A Christian?

ARCHIE: No, a Nazi.

JASON: A Nazi?

ARCHIE: Yeah.

JASON: OK, whatever you say. But you, you of all people, bringing up God?

ARCHIE: At this point, who else? Nietzsche?

Both laugh, heartily.

JASON: That's funny, Archie.

ARCHIE: Perhaps a philosophy lecturer's joke—but I'm also serious.

JASON: Really?

ARCHIE: Yeah. You know, I once translated Kant's *Foundation of the Metaphysics of Morals*. Now, to translate Kant you have to be into hardcore philosophy.

JASON: If you say so.

ARCHIE: But during all those years in my work and study, I always had this strong sense of the utter fruitlessness of it all. And since being here, with these lights flickering overhead . . .

JASON: Ask not for whom the light flickers—

ARCHIE: Exactly. It's like, no matter how unshakable their first principles or how logical their systems, in the end . . .

JASON: In the end?

ARCHIE: In the end, all those philosophers are dead and everyone who reads them will be dead . . . So I think I know what Heidegger meant.

JASON: You sound like Preacher Mike.

ARCHIE: Maybe you ought to listen to him next time he comes. Be a little nicer to him.

JASON: Even if I don't believe what he says?

ARCHIE: So what?

JASON: So just believe because it will make me feel better?

ARCHIE: Why not?

JASON: Are we that desperate?

ARCHIE: *(Glancing at the clock.)* You tell me, Jason.

Archie steps away from the bars and sits on his bed. As if taking a cue from Archie, Jason sits on his.

JASON: Only a God can save us, huh?

ARCHIE: You have a better option?

JASON: I don't know.

ARCHIE: Don't know what?

JASON: All I ever wanted was a sense of purpose for my life, that's all. Was that too much to ask for?

ARCHIE: You wouldn't think so.

JASON: I thought I had found it, too.

ARCHIE: *(Leaning forward on his bed and speaking louder.)* You did, Jason, you did. And that was fine for you then. The situation changed and now you need to move on.

JASON: Is that supposed to be funny?

ARCHIE: You know what I mean.

JASON: OK. So I move on. I find something else in my last few hours. Like what . . . God?

ARCHIE: Whatever works for you, whatever makes you feel better, and if that's God, fine. Though, I have to admit, in your situation, I can't think of anything else.

JASON: If I couldn't live believing a lie, Archie, why should I die believing one?

ARCHIE: Everyone lives and dies in lies.

JASON: If everything is a lie, what you're telling me is a lie too, so why should I believe it?

ARCHIE: *(Archie lies down on the bed.)* I'm not telling you to believe anything.

JASON: No?

ARCHIE: No, I'm just trying to help.

JASON: *(Jason gets up, goes to the bars and grabs two.)* Look at the bars of your cell, Archie.

ARCHIE: *(Not getting up, he turns his head.)* OK.

JASON: You looking?

ARCHIE: I said yes.

JASON: Sometimes I don't feel real. Sometimes I think my life is a just a dream.

ARCHIE: I know the feeling.

JASON: But these bars are the most real things I have ever known—ever! *(He pounds them.)* Yet one day, one day they're going to be gone. The bars, Archie, even these bars aren't going to last. *(He pounds them harder.)*

ARCHIE: Maybe that's what Heidegger meant. If these bars aren't going to last, what about us?

JASON: *(Falling into the bars.)* That's the point.

ARCHIE: That was Heidegger's, too.

JASON: Can you be saved by a God you don't believe in, Archie?

ARCHIE: If you want.

Jason drops back on his bed.

JASON: Your philosophy doesn't work—at least not for me.

ARCHIE: Why not?

JASON: Because I need something more objective.

ARCHIE: *(He snickers, his head still turned.)* Objective? How objective?

JASON: *(Gets up and stands at the bars.)* Something as objective as the fact that in less than seven hours my body is going to be strapped into the electric chair. Then, when some government official flips a switch and 2000 volts ram into me, steam will start pouring out of my holes, I might break a few bones flailing, I might catch on fire and my eyeballs could pop out of my sockets. When it's over, my tissues will have swelled, my skin will be red because my body will be too hot to touch and my brains will be cooked.

Still on the bed, Archie turns his head away from the bars. He says nothing.

JASON: Something that objective, OK, Archie? Give me something that objective.

Archie doesn't respond.

(End of Act Two)

Act Three

Same scene. Clock reads "1:00" and continues to count down. Jason stands, his arms dangling through the bars. Archie sleeps, lightly snoring.

JASON: Wake up.

Archie stirs but the snoring resumes.

JASON: Wake up!

Startled, Archie stumbles out of the bed and falls into the bars.

ARCHIE: Wha— wha—?

JASON: Sorry to disturb you.

ARCHIE: Yeah, yeah . . .

JASON: But I thought you might want to look at the clock.

Archie, glancing up, gasps.

ARCHIE: No, that can't be.

JASON: It can't be—but it is.

ARCHIE: Why . . . why didn't you get me up?

JASON: I did.

ARCHIE: Earlier, earlier?

JASON: You seemed so peaceful. Besides, I know you like dreams.

ARCHIE: Just the ones in which I'm free.

JASON: The exact ones I hate because when I wake up I'm here.

ARCHIE: Only an hour left? I can't believe I slept all this time!

JASON: Don't sweat it. What are we other than just shadows to each other, anyway?

ARCHIE: Don't say that.

JASON: It's true.

ARCHIE: *(Shaking the bars.)* This isn't right!

JASON: What isn't?

ARCHIE: You dying.

JASON: Everybody is dying.

ARCHIE: We have to do something!

JASON: *(He laughs bitterly.)* What? Call my lawyer? We saw what good that did.

ARCHIE: But you're innocent.

The lights flash. Both stand silently until they stop.

JASON: Maybe 67007 was, too?

ARCHIE: I can't just stand here.

JASON: Then lie down again. Besides, what are you going to do? Call Warden Ivan and tell him I confessed to a crime my now-deceased ex-wife committed? I'm sure he's going to get all worked up over that.

ARCHIE: We have to try.

JASON: Drop it—please.

Archie's about to protest when prison guard Stokes enters, along with a guard carrying a tray. They walk to Jason's cell.

STOKES: This is for you, 45523.

Jason steps back as Stokes opens the cell and both enter. The other guard hooks the tray on the bars and they leave, Stokes locking the door.

JASON: Thanks.

STOKES: Any time.

JASON: Stokes?

STOKES: Yeah?

JASON: Where's Bennifer? I thought he was scheduled to be here today.

STOKES: You haven't heard?

JASON: Heard what?

STOKES: Bennifer's dead.

JASON: Dead?

STOKES: Heart attack. Got off his shift yesterday
and keeled over in the parking lot. Next
to a dumpster. He must have been lying
there for an hour before the garbage man
found him.

JASON: You're kidding?

STOKES: Nope. Kind of ironic, isn't it? You outlived
him. *(He glances at the meal.)* Don't let
it get cold.

Stokes and the other guard leave.

JASON: Can you believe it?

ARCHIE: Why not?

JASON: Bennifer dead?

ARCHIE: It happens.

JASON: I know what you're thinking. You're thinking
it's my fault.

ARCHIE: No, I'm not.

JASON: Then what are you thinking?

ARCHIE: Nothing—except that we're fools to build
hope on anything other than what feels
right for the moment, and the moment
it stops feeling right, we better move on.
Maybe if Bennifer had done it, he'd be
serving your . . . your last meal.

JASON: I can't believe he's dead.

ARCHIE: I wouldn't be worrying about Bennifer right now. I'd be eating my last . . . *(he starts to choke up)* my last meal.

After standing silently for a long moment, Jason pulls the chair in his cell to the tray. He sits, staring at the single bowl. With a disgusted look, he starts eating. After the first mouthful, he gags but keeps shovelling mouthfuls in.

ARCHIE: What are you eating?

JASON: *(Looking up, his mouth full.)* Cooked onions.

ARCHIE: I thought that's what I smelled. Why are you gagging?

JASON: They make me sick.

ARCHIE: Sick? Then why did you request them?

JASON: *(After gagging.)* You think I wanted my last meal to be good?

ARCHIE: What?

JASON: Cooked onions are what I smelled the day I was waiting for my dad—the day I knew he was never coming home. *(Gagging.)* This helps me remember how bitter the life I'm leaving really is.

Jason continues eating. Archie leans into the bars and begins to breathe heavily through his nose.

JASON: What are you doing?

Ignoring him, Archie continues breathing loudly. Jason repeats the question.

JASON: What are you doing?

ARCHIE: I always loved cooked onions. Just loved them. . . . Oh, God, I don't want to die! I don't want to die!

JASON: I don't either, but what else is there if you don't want to live?

ARCHIE: *(Between breaths.)* I'd do anything for a bowl of cooked onions now.

JASON: You want mine?

ARCHIE: Yes! *(Suddenly paying attention to Jason.)* Is it a plastic bowl you can squeeze through the bars so I can grab it? *(He moves to the corner.)* Can you?

JASON: It's thick plastic. I can't get it through.

ARCHIE: Then why did you offer it?

JASON: Just wanted to see if you'd take it—the last meal of a condemned man.

ARCHIE: They were making you sick!

JASON: Yeah, yeah.

Archie drops back on his bed. Jason gags through a few more mouthfuls before stopping.

JASON: Archie?

ARCHIE: What?

JASON: You mad?

ARCHIE: I ought to be but I'm not.

JASON: Good . . . Archie?

ARCHIE: What?

JASON: I'm getting scared.

Archie stands up and goes back to the bars. Jason gets up and goes to the bars, too.

ARCHIE: I'm three months away and I'm scared.

JASON: I'm thinking about things. . . . Nothing like staring death in the face to get you thinking.

ARCHIE: Tell me about it.

JASON: You know, when I was kid, about five or six, my mum took me to my granddad's funeral. After the funeral, we were in the parking lot and I asked my mum about how long death was.

ARCHIE: What did she say?

JASON: I don't remember exactly but I have an image in my mind of this infinite blackness or something. No matter which direction you looked in or how fast you went or how long you went, the blackness never ended, never changed, never left.

ARCHIE: That's pleasant.

JASON: It was horrifying. Sometimes I thought I just dreamed the whole thing, the funeral and image of blackness—but it never left me. And now, this same image—this infinite blackness that never ends—it keeps coming back. *(He lightly bangs his head against the bars.)* I can see and feel it now.

ARCHIE: I've seen and felt it, too.

JASON: Really?

ARCHIE: Really.

JASON: It's all crazy.

ARCHIE: I know.

JASON: Maybe the purpose of life is to keep ourselves too busy to think about our death. Have you ever thought about that?

ARCHIE: I don't know. I guess I've thought about everything at some point.

JASON: But now—now there's not enough life left to preoccupy me. Death is like right in front of me, this big dark thing that swallows up everything.

ARCHIE: I've seen that big dark thing, too. It's out there.

JASON: Are there any answers that death doesn't negate?

ARCHIE: *(Shaking his head.)* There ought to be.

JASON: Come on, you and your philosophy should have something for me other than a shadow with a shaking head. Are there any answers that death doesn't just steamroll over?

ARCHIE: I don't know of any.

JASON: No?

ARCHIE: Not without God.

JASON: God? You back at him again?

ARCHIE: When it comes to death, I don't see anything else.

JASON: Not Nietzsche? Or . . . or that Nazi?

ARCHIE: Heidegger?

JASON: Yeah.

ARCHIE: No, not Nietzsche or the Nazi.

JASON: *(Shaking his head.)* It's so, so weird.

ARCHIE: What?

JASON: Here I am, minutes away from death, and you know what I'm thinking about?

ARCHIE: No.

JASON: I'm thinking about my dad.

ARCHIE: Your dad?

JASON: For some reason, I keep thinking, if only my dad came that day, if only he had come and we went on the boat and caught that sailfish . . . then, then all this would be alright, it really would.

ARCHIE: Well . . .

JASON: I have this image of him and me on the boat. And the sailfish dancing on its tail, and my dad grabbing the fishing pole, and his muscles bulging, and him reeling it in, all wet and glistening in the salty sun, and its tail and bill whacking the deck after we get him on board. And everyone on the boat is looking over at us and taking pictures. And there we would be—my dad and me—and I would be so proud because everyone would know that this was my dad and that we caught the sailfish. If only that happened, just a guy and his dad catching a sailfish, nothing more . . .

ARCHIE: Sure.

JASON: Here I am—facing death—and all I can think about is something that never happened. Does that make sense?

ARCHIE: About as much as anything.

JASON: Right now it seems like death is going to suck everything into the ground. Unless . . .

ARCHIE: Unless?

JASON: Unless death itself is the answer. Have you ever thought of that, Archie?

ARCHIE: No.

JASON: Yeah, maybe death itself is the answer.

ARCHIE: If that works for you.

Jason laughs.

ARCHIE: What's so funny?

JASON: You just said it so unenthusiastically, as if you really didn't believe it.

ARCHIE: I don't know what I believe. I believe in nothing.

JASON: I know at least one thing you believe in.

ARCHIE: What's that?

JASON: That in a little while they're going to come down and strap me in the electric chair and before long the guy you have been talking to for five years will be dead. You believe in that at least, don't you?

Archie stands silently.

JASON: Come on, you believe in that, right? Tell me, tell me, Archie, "Whatever works best for you" — or something like that. Just say it with a little conviction, something to help me along here.

ARCHIE: We need to stop this execution.

JASON: But if we can't, then what? Tell me, Archie, tell me . . . *(Jason looks at the floor.)* That's all you have for me, a motionless shadow?

A guard enters. Another man, dressed in a casual suit, follows. He's in his early forties: Preacher Mike. His hair is long, in a pony tail, with streaks of grey. The guard sets the chair down outside Jason's cell and tells him to get no closer. The man sits as the guard leaves.

PREACHER MIKE: Hello, brother. I know that you didn't ask for me to come but I did anyway. I hope that it's agreeable . . . Jason, are you alright?

Jason stares at him.

ARCHIE: He's not doing great, Reverend.

PREACHER MIKE: I can see that. I wondered how well he'd hold up . . .

JASON: *(Leaning through the bars.)* Do you have any answers, preacher?

PREACHER MIKE: What?

JASON: I said, Do you have answers? My roommate here has nothing. Nothing — a shadow with a shaking head.

PREACHER MIKE: I, I—

JASON: I'm facing death in a few minutes and I need answers.

PREACHER MIKE: This is a change—

JASON: Answers, preacher, answers!

PREACHER MIKE: *(Pulling his chair closer.)* Answers? Why, yes—

JASON: You do? So answer me this. I've had a pathetic life, accomplished little good and now it's all heading with me into a hole in the ground. So what does this all mean, preacher?

PREACHER MIKE: Your life—what does it mean?

JASON: Yeah, what does it mean if it ends in death?

PREACHER MIKE: Sure, well, Jason, for starters, we have to try and keep everything in perspective.

JASON: Perspective?

PREACHER MIKE: Yes, we have to keep our lives in perspective, that is, in congruence with the bigger picture.

JASON: Like what?

PREACHER MIKE: Like God.

JASON: Of course. How silly of me. What else did I expect a preacher to say? Fine. I mean, desperate times call for desperate measures, huh?

PREACHER MIKE: We're all in a bit of a desperate situation, wouldn't you say, Jason?

JASON: But not as desperate as mine.

PREACHER: No—at least not now, though eventually we all face death.

JASON: OK, God, fine. But how do I know this God even exists?

PREACHER MIKE: The Scriptures say that—

JASON: Forget the Scriptures. How do I know that this God is real?

PREACHER MIKE: OK, brother, that's a fair enough question. So let me start with a simple assumption.

JASON: Please hurry.

PREACHER MIKE: My assumption is this—something undeniably exists.

JASON: Huh?

PREACHER MIKE: Something undeniably exists.

JASON: What are you talking about?

ARCHIE: Listen to him, Jason. That's his first assumption—"Something undeniably exists." He's going to build an argument from there.

JASON: OK, something undeniably exists—like these bars?

PREACHER MIKE: Like these bars.

JASON: And like the electric chair down the hall?

PREACHER MIKE: Unfortunately.

JASON: OK.

PREACHER MIKE: Now, is it possible that these bars or even that electric chair could not exist? That is, their non-existence is a possibility, correct? There wouldn't be any logical conundrum by them not existing.

JASON: That's for sure.

PREACHER MIKE: Now, these things did not come into existence by themselves, correct? Something else had to make them.

JASON: Like these bars?

PREACHER MIKE: Correct. These bars didn't create themselves—

JASON: Nor did the electric chair.

PREACHER MIKE: Correct. Something else had to. So anything that does not have to exist but does exist is caused by something else, something before it.

JASON: It would have to exist, in order to make it.

PREACHER MIKE: Correct, so whatever created these bars existed before the bars.

JASON: Correct, correct—but get to the point.

PREACHER MIKE: I'm trying. Now, whatever was before the bars and created them had also to be created by something before it, and whatever created that was created by something before that.

JASON: OK.

PREACHER MIKE: But this cannot go on back forever in an infinite regress of events.

JASON: What?

PREACHER MIKE: Things can't keep going on backwards forever.

JASON: Why not?

ARCHIE: It's called the impossibility of traversing the infinite, Jason. Listen to him.

JASON: The what?

ARCHIE: The impossibility of traversing the infinite. It's like trying to count to zero from the largest negative number possible, from negative infinity to zero. It can't be done. You can't have an infinite number of actual events.

JASON: OK? Whatever . . . ?

ARCHIE: Look at it this way—you don't mind me interrupting here, do you, Reverend?

PREACHER MIKE: No, please, continue.

ARCHIE: If something started at some infinite time in the past, we'd never reach where we are now, because how could an infinity of time have passed in order to get us here. You understand?

JASON: Well, I guess . . . go on.

PREACHER MIKE: Good, brother. Now, if there can't be an infinite regress of events, something had to start everything, a first cause, something that itself wasn't caused but always existed and was before all things.

JASON: God, I take it?

PREACHER MIKE: Yes, brother, God—the God described in the Holy Scriptures. That's why I believe He exists.

Jason looks up at the clock.

JASON: OK, preacher, you win. Your God exists. Hallelujah!

PREACHER MIKE: Jason—

JASON: No, I'm serious. Something had to start it all and what else could that be but God?

PREACHER MIKE: OK—

JASON: But unless this God performs some miracle on my behalf, I have only a few minutes left! So what good does this God—this "first-cause" God—do me?

PREACHER MIKE: This leads to Jesus.

JASON: Jesus?

PREACHER MIKE: Yes, Jesus.

JASON: Jesus? OK, what else should a preacher be talking about?

PREACHER MIKE: I believe that this, as you called Him, first-cause God took on Himself human flesh. That is, the Creator of the universe, the One who created all things, became a human being and lived on this earth for 33 years, then died as a sacrifice for all our sins.

JASON: God, the power that Created the universe, became a human being?

PREACHER MIKE: Correct.

JASON: And that's Jesus?

PREACHER MIKE: Correct.

JASON: That's pretty wild. But what does it mean for me?

PREACHER MIKE: It means that if you have faith in Him, that if you truly believe in Him and His death for you, then you can have the promise of eternal life right now.

JASON: Just believe in Him?

PREACHER MIKE: If what I've said is true and the Creator of the universe did take on human flesh and then died in that flesh, do you think that there's anything you could do to add to that?

JASON: I guess not.

PREACHER MIKE: That's why it comes to us as a gift, by faith alone.

JASON: But how does that give any meaning to my life?

PREACHER MIKE: Because your life is not so different from anyone else's, Jason. No matter how long we live or what we do, it all ends in death.

JASON: We were just talking about that before you came. Weren't we, Archie?

PREACHER MIKE: But the whole purpose of the gospel is to beat death.

JASON: Beat death?

PREACHER MIKE: Correct. Though we die, we have the promise of something afterward—a resurrection to a new life. Jesus beat death and He offers that victory to anyone who accepts it by faith.

Jason steps back and falls on his bed.

JASON: I'm supposed to believe this?

PREACHER MIKE: It's your only hope, brother.

JASON: But this Jesus isn't going to save me from the electric chair, is He?

PREACHER MIKE: He gives you something beyond it.

JASON: *(Letting out a long sigh.)* Preacher Mike?

PREACHER MIKE: Yes, Jason.

JASON: Let me ask you a simple question.

PREACHER MIKE: Sure, go ahead.

JASON: Why would your God die "for all our sins"?

PREACHER MIKE: Because He loves us. And He loves you, Jason.

JASON: *(Getting back up and returning to the bars.)* He loves me?

PREACHER MIKE: Correct.

JASON: That's nice.

PREACHER MIKE: It's more than nice.

JASON: This God loves me?

PREACHER MIKE: Very much.

JASON: OK, if He loves me "very much," how come I'm about to be strapped into an electric chair and have thousands of volts of electricity cook me like a barbecued pig?

PREACHER MIKE: That gets into another area.

JASON: No, come on, now. If I love someone and they are about to be electrocuted, and if I have the power to stop it—if I'm God or something—I would stop it!

PREACHER MIKE: It's not that simple.

JASON: Yes it is! It's as simple as the fact that I'm going to die a pretty wretched death and your loving God isn't going to do a thing about it, which I would understand if He hated me. But if He loves me, why doesn't He stop these men who are probably getting ready now to take me away?

PREACHER MIKE: I don't have a full answer on that—

JASON: You said you had answers.

PREACHER MIKE: I do, I do, but I don't have complete answers on everything, not on all the details.

JASON: *(Letting out a howl.)* Details? Well, excuse me, preacher, but maybe my death is a detail in your busy schedule, but it's not a detail to me.

PREACHER MIKE: No, Jason, I meant only that some of the bad things that happen we just don't have answers for. But we can trust

God that all things will eventually work out for good.

JASON: *(Sarcastically.)* Wonderful, just wonderful.

PREACHER MIKE: Brother, please . . .

JASON: So you can't explain to me why, if God loves me, He's going to allow them to fry me? Is that what you are saying?

PREACHER MIKE: God loves us but we often have to face the consequences of our actions.

JASON: Oh, yeah?

PREACHER MIKE: And though I have strong feelings about the death penalty, I do believe that the Lord can sometimes work through the justice system.

JASON: Really now?

PREACHER MIKE: Yes. And, brother, though you can be forgiven by God right now, you did commit a pretty heinous crime—

ARCHIE: Uh, oh!

Jason lets out a deep sarcastic laugh.

PREACHER MIKE: Did I say something funny?

JASON: *(Sarcastically.)* Did you say something funny? Did he say something funny, Archie?

PREACHER MIKE: I don't understand.

JASON: Tell him, Archie. Tell him how his loving God sometimes works through the justice system.

PREACHER MIKE: What am I missing here?

JASON: This is rich, so rich. Tell him, Archie, I don't have the heart to.

PREACHER MIKE: Tell me what?

ARCHIE: There's been a rather late-breaking development in Jason's case, Reverend.

PREACHER MIKE: There has?

ARCHIE: Yeah—and you're probably not going to believe it.

PREACHER MIKE: What?

ARCHIE: I found out less than a day ago, but it appears that Jason's confession, the one about shooting that kid in the back of the neck and all, was a lie.

PREACHER MIKE: A lie?

ARCHIE: He's innocent, Reverend.

PREACHER MIKE: Innocent?

ARCHIE: That's right. So unless some miracle comes from above, an innocent man is about to be sent to the electric chair.

PREACHER MIKE: Wait, I'm confused. *(Looking toward Jason.)* You had confessed to this crime years ago, correct?

JASON: Correct.

PREACHER MIKE: But you didn't do it?

JASON: Correct.

PREACHER MIKE: Why did you confess?

JASON: I don't know.

PREACHER MIKE: You don't know?

ARCHIE: He confessed to save his wife. She committed the crime.

PREACHER WIFE: Your wife?

JASON: Afraid so.

ARCHIE: But he just found out that she killed herself. And so now he's having second thoughts about everything. Why go to the chair for someone who's dead? It's a bit of a pickle, hey Reverend?

PREACHER MIKE: I don't believe this.

ARCHIE: I told you you wouldn't.

PREACHER MIKE: If this is a way to avoid your sentence, it's a bit late, isn't it?

ARCHIE: Trust me, Reverend, it's not that.

PREACHER MIKE: No?

ARCHIE: No. I mean, he all but wants to die. He's

just looking for a few answers on the way out, that's all.

PREACHER MIKE: Jason, are you saying to me that you didn't commit the crime they are about to execute you for?

JASON: You got it, preacher.

PREACHER MIKE: This can't be!

JASON: It can't be—but it is.

PREACHER MIKE: This is . . . very disturbing, to say the least.

JASON: To say the least.

PREACHER MIKE: Innocent?

JASON: Yes, innocent. So it appears that God is about to let me die for a crime I didn't commit. But He loves me "very much" all the same, correct?

PREACHER MIKE: This can't be.

JASON: You got any answers for me now, preacher?

PREACHER MIKE: Answers?

JASON: That would be nice.

PREACHER MIKE: Answers?

JASON: If you don't mind.

PREACHER MIKE: The cross.

JASON: The what?

PREACHER MIKE: The cross, Jason, the cross.

JASON: That's your answer?

PREACHER MIKE: Yes, that's it! That's the explanation! At the cross, the greatest injustice ever took place, the innocent God dying for guilty humanity. No injustice anyone ever faces will match that.

JASON: But what does that have to do with me?

PREACHER MIKE: I, I don't . . . know.

JASON: You don't know?

PREACHER MIKE: All I can say is that because of the cross, we have hope that justice will be done.

JASON: When? In heaven or something?

PREACHER MIKE: When else?

JASON: Oh, come on!

PREACHER MIKE: When else, Jason? If it doesn't come then, it will never come because it doesn't come here. Without that hope, there is no hope.

Preacher Mike gets up and moves toward the bars. He stops a few feet away.

JASON: That's all you have for me, some hope of an afterlife? Some hope from a God who is supposed to bring all this justice in eternity but can't or won't now?

Preacher Mike stands. Jason stares back in silence.

PREACHER MIKE: Jason.

JASON: What?

PREACHER MIKE: Can I pray with you?

JASON: Pray with me? Oh, just wonderful. *(He snickers.)* Did you hear that, Archie? Preacher Mike wants to pray with me. That's so kind of you, preacher, it really is. Why didn't we think of this earlier? Then everything would be solved.

PREACHER MIKE: *(Stepping a little closer.)* May I?

JASON: No! Stay away from me. You were supposed to have answers and you have nothing.

PREACHER MIKE: Jason, please.

JASON: No! . . . OK, wait a minute. Sure, you can pray for me.

PREACHER MIKE: I can?

JASON: Yes, but on one condition. You can pray right now that your God, your Jesus, will spare me from the electric chair, but before you do, you have to guarantee me that He will answer that prayer and I will be spared.

PREACHER MIKE: Jason—

JASON: No, you have to guarantee me that He will answer that prayer.

PREACHER MIKE: I—

JASON: You what? What else is worth praying for right now, other than that an innocent man not be killed? And yet if you can't guarantee me that He will spare me, why should I waste my last few minutes listening to a prayer that won't get answered?

PREACHER MIKE: Jason, I—

JASON: What?

PREACHER MIKE: *(Shaking his head.)* I can't, as much as I wish I could. But what I can do is—

JASON: I don't want to hear it. If you can't do that for me, you have nothing for me and I want you to go.

PREACHER MIKE: Jason, listen. It's not that simple—

JASON: No! Either do what I ask or go.

PREACHER MIKE: Jason, please—

JASON: No, go away!

Stymied and shaken, Preacher Mike gets up and leaves. A long silence hovers in the air.

JASON: "Only a God can save us"?

ARCHIE: I didn't say some preacher could. But what a story.

JASON: Story?

ARCHIE: The Jesus thing. God, the Creator of the universe, becoming a man, suffering worse than any person suffered, suffering an injustice worse than any of us can suffer? Incredible! I forgot that's what Christians believe.

JASON: Did he convert you?

ARCHIE: Imagine, though, if it were true. God so relating to us that He dies with us, as a human being? What a different spin that puts on things!

JASON: But suppose it's not true?

ARCHIE: It ought to be, then.

JASON: Archie.

ARCHIE: *(Still enraptured.)* It ought to be . . .

JASON: Archie!

ARCHIE: Huh?

JASON: They're going to be here any minute now.

ARCHIE: I know, I know.

JASON: It's too late.

ARCHIE: No, we have to stop it. Guard! Guard! Guard! *(He picks up a cup from his sink and bangs it on the bars.)* Guard! Guard!

JASON: *(Yelling over the noise.)* What are you doing?

Prison Guard Stokes comes in. His baton is drawn.

STOKES: What is going on?

ARCHIE: *(Still banging the cup.)* We have to do
something! He's innocent! He's innocent!

STOKES: Stop the banging!

ARCHIE: Jason's innocent—and they're about to put
him in the chair!

Stokes slams the baton on the bars.

STOKES: Stop!

ARCHIE: *(He stops banging the cup.)* He's innocent!
He's innocent!

STOKES: If you don't calm down, we're going to lock
you in solitary!

ARCHIE: *(Practically in tears.)* But, but he is . . .

STOKES: Sure, sure.

ARCHIE: He is!

STOKES: Quiet down.

ARCHIE: He's about to . . . die.

STOKES: We're all about to die, 69691. Some are just
early achievers, that's all. Now shut up!

Archie calms down but sniffles loudly.

STOKES: That's better. I'm telling you, don't get me back in here again or you will be sorry.

Stokes steps back and, as he's about to leave, he hesitates, moves toward Jason's cell and looks at him.

STOKES: You innocent?

JASON: *(After a few seconds.)* Yeah.

STOKES: Really?

JASON: Yeah.

STOKES: *(Putting the baton back in his belt, he glances at Jason.)* I believe you.

JASON: You do?

STOKES: Yeah, I do. *(He glances at the clock.)* Too bad. It happens sometimes.

Stokes leaves. Jason and Archie stand at the bars. Neither speaks for a few moments.

JASON: They're coming.

ARCHIE: No! No! No!

JASON: I felt so ready before.

ARCHIE: Don't think like that.

JASON: They're coming, and all I can do is think about my dad and that sailfish . . . Look at my shadow, Archie. In just a little while, I won't even be a shadow on the floor anymore—not even a shadow.

ARCHIE: This can't be happening.

JASON: It's like a dream.

ARCHIE: Maybe it's all a dream.

JASON: Should shadows be scared?

ARCHIE: No, because they're nothing, an absence of something.

JASON: That's my life, an absence of something. And now, there's going to be even less . . . Archie. Archie, I hear them coming! *(Squeezing himself into the bars.)* They're coming!

A prison guard enters with two men. Both are in suits. One is short and stocky, with thick black hair, Detective Frank Spinolo. The other is tall, thin and blonde. He's carrying a briefcase. He's Archie's lawyer, Richard Stern. They stand outside Archie's cell. Both have gleeful, excited looks. The prison guard leaves.

ARCHIE: Richard? Detective Spinolo? Wow!

RICHARD: Hello, Archie!

ARCHIE: Hello to you. What is this?

RICHARD: We have incredible news.

ARCHIE: News?

RICHARD: About your case.

ARCHIE: My case?

95

RICHARD: Good news. Very good news.

ARCHIE: You mean it?

RICHARD: You think we'd be joking? I thought Frank here should be the first to tell you because, without him, it wouldn't have happened.

SPINOLO: Hello, Archie.

ARCHIE: Hello, Detective. What's—what's going on?

SPINOLO: As you know, Archie, from the start I never believed you were guilty.

ARCHIE: Yes.

SPINOLO: Vega—he was my man, from day one. I never gave up, either. I used to lie in bed at night and tell my wife, "Sadie, I'm going to get that innocent man out of jail, no matter what." Well, old Judge Waxman finally died and there was a new judge, Maxine Carter. I hounded and hounded her, we showed her more evidence and finally got her to agree to the DNA tests.

ARCHIE: You got the tests!

SPINOLO: We got 'em!

ARCHIE: And?

SPINOLO: Like you said all along, they fingered Vega for your wife's murder.

ARCHIE: You're kidding?

SPINOLO: Hardly. We just got the warrant for his arrest for the murder of Mrs Archibald McDonald. I'd have arrested him myself but wanted to come with Richard and tell you the news. Vega's probably being charged as we speak.

ARCHIE: For real? For real?

SPINOLO: For real, my friend, for real!

RICHARD: You're going free, Archie!

ARCHIE: Free!

RICHARD: Within the next few minutes, once a few papers from the governor's office get signed by the warden's office, you'll be out of here.

ARCHIE: I can't believe it!

RICHARD: Believe it!

ARCHIE: They did the test. I can't believe it!

RICHARD: What's more, we're probably going to file suit against the state. It owes you something, after all this.

ARCHIE: I can't believe it.

SPINOLO: Why not? There's a God in heaven, isn't there? And He loves justice, doesn't He? And so do I. It was a little late in coming, but it's justice. Congratulations!

RICHARD: Yes, Archie, congratulations!

They hug each other through the bars. Spinolo and Richard are both in tears.

SPINOLO: I believed in you all along. Thank God.
That's all I can say, thank God.

ARCHIE: I can't believe it.

RICHARD: You will in a few minutes when the warden
lets you out.

ARCHIE: This is like a dream.

SPINOLO: Dreams don't get this good.

RICHARD: We're going back to the warden's office
now—try to hurry him along with the
papers.

ARCHIE: That's great!

RICHARD: They said something about an execution
in a few minutes and he might be tied
up. I'm going to try to push him to do it
before. We want you out of here as soon
as possible and we want to be here when
they open your cell door.

SPINOLO: I even brought my camera, to sneak a
quick picture.

ARCHIE: Are you sure this isn't a mistake—some
kind of error?

RICHARD: No, we got everything we needed, from the governor down. You're a free man. All they need to do is open the door.

ARCHIE: How can I thank you?

SPINOLO: No need to. We're just doing our job.

RICHARD: We'll be back in a few minutes. Don't go anywhere.

They all laugh, then both men leave. Archie and Jason stand at the bars.

ARCHIE: I'm going to be free! I'm going free! I, I—

He stops. Having forgotten about Jason, he now remembers. He looks down at Jason's shadow, which doesn't move.

JASON: I heard.

ARCHIE: What can I say?

JASON: There's nothing to say.

ARCHIE: I'm reeling.

JASON: I guess so.

ARCHIE: I'm going to speak to the warden, Jason, as soon as he comes down.

JASON: That's a nice gesture, but it's too late . . . Besides, you heard him, they wanted to do the next execution first. That must be me.

ARCHIE: When the warden comes, I'm going to plead for you. I'm going to tell him the truth—that you are innocent and that you should be freed, too.

Jason laughs.

ARCHIE: What's so funny?

JASON: What you said.

ARCHIE: What did I say?

JASON: Forget it.

ARCHIE: Tell me.

JASON: When you said that I should be freed, too. Too?

ARCHIE: Yes, you should—

Archie stops, as if the implications of Jason's words just strike him.

JASON: It's OK, Archie, I'm glad for you . . . I guess I'd just be gladder if an innocent man wasn't going to die instead.

ARCHIE: Shhhh!

JASON: I just know what an innocent man feels like when he's about to be executed.

ARCHIE: *(Looking around.)* Will you be careful? What's wrong with you?

JASON: But as you've been saying all along now,

you got to do what makes you feel good, even if that means someone else going down for you.

ARCHIE: Quiet!

JASON: Don't worry, Archie, your secret's safe. After all, the only one who knows it is soon going to be dead.

ARCHIE: Be care—

Five guards walk in, followed by a large black man with white hair in a grey suit, Warden Ivan. They stop outside Jason's cell. The guards allow the warden to approach the bars.

WARDEN IVAN: 45523?

Standing at the bars, Jason says nothing.

WARDEN IVAN: 45523, please step back from the cell door.

Jason doesn't move.

WARDEN IVAN: 45523, I am ordering you to step back. Please don't make this more difficult than it need be.

Instead of stepping back, Jason wraps himself around the bars so the cell door can't be opened. Warden Ivan nods to the guards, who move forward. Two take out their batons and try to pry him loose.

JASON: *(Screaming.)* No, no! I am innocent, I am

innocent! I didn't do it, I didn't do it!

When they finally get him away from the door, a guard unlocks it and pushes the door open. Jason grabs the corner of his bed, still screaming. Four guards wrestle him up, handcuffing him behind his back, then shuffle him out.

JASON: No, no, I didn't do it! My wife did it, my wife did it! My confession was a lie! It was a lie!

WARDEN IVAN: Calm down, 45523!

JASON: I didn't do it! I swear, I didn't! I didn't!

They walk Jason past Archie's cell. Jason forces them to stop. He and Archie stare, seeing each other face-to-face for the first time in years.

JASON: Tell them, Archie! Tell them what I told you! Tell them I'm innocent.

Archie stands in silence.

JASON: What are you doing? Tell them!

Archie says nothing.

JASON: Archie? Archie? How can you stand there? Tell them, tell them!

Archie remains silent.

JASON: I won't say anything. I swear, I won't! Tell them!

WARDEN IVAN: Enough is enough. Move!

The guards shuffle Jason offstage. Warden Ivan remains behind and turns the countdown clock off.

JASON: *(Yelling from offstage, repeatedly.)* Archie's guilty! Archie murdered his wife, he told me, he told me!

Stokes, Spinolo and Richard enter. Spinolo looks over his shoulder, toward the cries. All stop in front of Archie's cell.

WARDEN IVAN: *(To Richard and Spinolo.)* Oh, yes, yes. I know you good men are looking for me. Understandable, understandable . . . Yes, yes, 69691, congratulations.

Archie nods.

WARDEN IVAN: Lucky you. Regrettable as it is, a few innocent ones slip through the cracks. Glad you won't be one. Makes my day to let an innocent one go. Yes, yes.

SPINOLO: What was that all about, that prisoner they were taking away?

WARDEN IVAN: He's on his way to the chair.

SPINOLO: Ouch!

WARDEN IVAN: Even the ones who confess, the ones in whom no question of their guilt exists—even they sometimes, as zero-hour approaches, claim innocence. Never would have expected it out of that one, though.

SPINOLO: He was claiming that Archie was guilty, that he confessed?

WARDEN IVAN: Never heard anyone do that before, start accusing another of guilt. But the prospect of death does strange things to people. Yes, yes.

ARCHIE: For sure. *(He sniggers.)* Poor 45523 was saying all sorts of crazy things toward the end there.

SPINOLO: Oh, yeah?

ARCHIE: Yeah, going crazy big time. Saying stuff about if only he and his dad had caught a sailfish, then he would be ready to die, and other crazy stuff.

SPINOLO: Really?

ARCHIE: Really, I mean wacko. 45523 was upset that I was getting released. Accusing me, claiming his own innocence, talking about that dumb sailfish.

WARDEN IVAN: I've seen some strange stuff before, but that was a first.

ARCHIE: He was really losing it. Admitted to killing that kid, then at the last minute claiming he was innocent. Never believed him, though, never.

STOKES: You didn't?

ARCHIE: *(Stunned by Stokes, as if he didn't expect him to say anything.)* Huh?

STOKES: You didn't believe him?

ARCHIE: No, no, of course not. He was going crazy.

STOKES: You seemed to a few minutes ago.

ARCHIE: Oh, yeah . . . all that. *(He sniggers.)* He kept on saying it and, as time was narrowing down, I was just desperate to try and calm him, that's all. Nothing more than that. I never believed him innocent.

STOKES: I do.

WARDEN IVAN: What Mr Stokes? You do what?

STOKES: I believe him to be innocent.

WARDEN IVAN: Now, Mr Stokes, please—

STOKES: No, I do. I believe he's innocent.

WARDEN IVAN: Why so, Mr Stokes?

STOKES: Just an intuition, nothing more.

WARDEN IVAN: Intuition, Mr Stokes?

STOKES: Yes, sir. Felt that way about 41121 last year. Turned out right.

WARDEN IVAN: Yes, yes, I remember now. Someone told me you thought he was innocent all along. Glad he was exonerated in time, too.

STOKES: The same with 98712.

WARDEN IVAN: Oh, yes, yes, 98712. The system was
a little late on that one, I'm afraid.

STOKES: I get this sense about who's innocent and
who's guilty.

WARDEN IVAN: Well, that's all very nice, Mr Stokes,
but—

STOKES: And 45523 was definitely innocent . . .

WARDEN IVAN: Well, fortunately, Mr Stokes, here we
follow the orders of the judicial system,
not the intuition of a guard. And now,
speaking of the judicial system . . . I know
a young man who needs to be released.
Mr Stokes, open Mr McDonald's cell.

Stokes hesitates for a moment.

WARDEN IVAN: Mr Stokes?

*Stokes goes over, opens the cell and steps back. Archie
walks out. He hugs Richard while Spinolo takes a pho-
tograph. He then hugs Spinolo while Richard takes a
photo. Archie shakes Warden Ivan's hand. There are
smiles, tears and laughter.*

WARDEN IVAN: It's not every day I get to release an
innocent man from death row. Yes, yes!

ARCHIE: Hooray!

WARDEN IVAN: I want to cherish the moment.

SPINOLO: Yahoo!

All three of them—Richard, Archie, and Spinolo—cheer a few times together, ending in wild laughter.

WARDEN IVAN: I'm supposed to be over at that execution, but I'd rather be here for this happy occasion. Not many happy occasions on death row.

RICHARD: This is the best day of my life.

ARCHIE: Mine, too!

Together all three, let out another cheer.

WARDEN IVAN: Mind if I try?

ALL THREE: Go ahead!

WARDEN IVAN: Hurray!

Everyone laughs.

RICHARD: Come on, let's get him out of here. I'm sure this is just what he wants to be doing, standing down here yelling—

All of them, including the Warden, cheer again, then break into laughter.

SPINOLO: You know what would be justice, after all this?

RICHARD: What's that?

SPINOLO: When they give Vega the death sentence,
I hope they put him in your cell, Archie.

RICHARD: Hurray!

WARDEN IVAN: I'll be waiting for this Mr Vega when
he comes.

SPINOLO: Maybe, Archie, you ought to write a little
note for him on the wall.

RICHARD: Yeah, welcome him to his new home.

ARCHIE: No way I'm going back in there!

Everyone laughs.

WARDEN IVAN: Let's go, gentlemen. Yes, yes, let's
go. I'm sure Mr McDonald here is more
than ready to go.

They start to exit, laughing as they do.

*The lights flicker. Everyone stops and falls silent. No-one
speaks. All four turn and look at Stokes, who—standing
by the cell door—slams it shut.*

(End of Play)